STEAM and RAIL in GERMANY

Edited by Paul Catchpole

A Locomotives International Publication

STEAM & RAIL IN GERMANY

FRONT COVER:
01 class Pacifics of both East and West Germany are represented here double-heading a special excursion between Nürnberg and Arnstadt. D.B. 01 150 is leading D.R. 01 531 as they approach Plaue in 1994.   Photo: Peter R.G. Kennard.

REAR COVER:
Spreewaldbahn metre gauge 0-6-0T 99 5703 outside the shed at Straupitz, north of Cottbus. The locomotive was built in 1897 by Hohenzollern, works no. 940, and was photographed on 5th July 1967, still at work. Seven locos of this design were built, of which 99 5703 survived to be preserved.   Photo: John K. Williams.

FRONTISPIECE:
An everyday scene of working steam in Germany as the Saarbrucken station pilot, D.B. 4-6-4T no. 078 062-7, prepares to haul carriages from an incoming local out of the station in October 1968.   Photo: Ian Thomson.

British Library Cataloguing in Publication Data. A catalogue record for this book is available from the British Library.

© 1998 *Locomotives International* and authors.
All rights reserved. No part of this book may be reproduced or transmitted in any form or by any means without prior written permission from the publisher.

ISBN 1-900340-06-2
First Edition. Published by Paul Catchpole Ltd., Kings Norton, Birmingham, England
Printed and bound by Neografia, Martin, Slovakia

STEAM AND RAIL IN GERMANY

Contents

A Brief History of German Railways

The development of steam and rail in Germany follows closely the gradual unification of a large quantity of states and principalities, and their subsequent joint histories. The first major alliance was the formation of a Teutonic Federation in 1815, followed by Zollverein (Customs Union) in 1834, coinciding with the onset of Germany's industrial revolution.

As in many other countries, coal mining formed the impetus for the application of steam power, and the first locomotive in Germany was built by the Royal Iron Foundry of Berlin for a mine railway in Silesia.

Public railway construction in Germany started in 1834 with the Ludwigsbahn, authorised by King Ludwig I of Bavaria and built over a four and a half mile route from Nürnberg to Fürth. The first locomotive on this railway was the 'Adler', a 2-2-2 built by Robert Stephenson in 1835, works number 118, and supplied with its driver, a Mr. Wilson. When the line opened to the public on 7th December 1835, Mr. Wilson was at the regulator for the inaugural trip from Fürth to Nürnberg. Although he had only been sent out see the 'Adler' through its trials, he married a German girl and stayed, becoming a well-known local character and enjoying the benefit of a salary said to be twice that of the General Manager! Goods were carried as well as passengers, and the first freight on the line was naturally a consignment of beer. In 1857 the 'Adler' was withdrawn and scrapped, but there are two replicas, one of which ran at Nürnberg for the 125th anniversary and is now housed in the Verkehrsmuseum near the station.

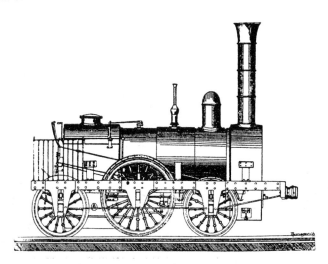

The Ludwigsbahn 2-2-2, 'Adler'

The next significant undertaking after the Ludwigsbahn was the Berlin - Potsdam line opened in 1837. This and other early railways were built in a Germany that was still a land of kingdom states. Most adopted the standard gauge of 1435 mm, with the exception of Baden, which constructed its lines to a gauge of 1600 mm. Baden eventually had to relent and was standardised in 1856.

The first international line was from Köln to Bruxelles via Aachen opened 1845, followed in 1857 by Frankfurt - Basle. The first Russian connection was made in 1860. The Russian border was much further east then than it is now, as eastern Prussia covered an area encompassing today's Baltic states.

Prussia recognised the military significance of railways early on and built lines with strategic use in mind. The railways played a significant part in the attack on Denmark in 1863 and were crucial to the Franco-Prussian War of 1870. Prussian locos were even built with top half of chimney removable so that they could work over foreign lines with a more restricted loading gauge.

After the Franco-Prussian war Alsace-Lorraine was gained, and with the extra territory included there were 12,000 miles of railway. The strength of Prussian influence led to the Unification of the Imperial German Empire in 1871, setting the scene for further rapid development.

In 1875 and 1878 laws were passed creating three specific types of secondary and minor railways. These consisted of the Nebenbahn, a regional state or private secondary line, sometimes also called Landesbahn; Kreisbahn, a local council railway at roughly equivalent to English county level; and the Lokalbahn, a local light railway or tramway.

Nebenbahn lines were of various gauges, but usually built to 1435 mm, and gauges generally diminished according to the area's wealth or the line's stature. Generally the gauges used were metre, 750 mm or 600 mm. The rules governing Kreisbahn and Lokalbahn railways only permitted operation at a maximum speed of 30 kph. The 600 mm gauge Feldbahn, or field railway, was a later product of the First World War, when light railways were needed to supply the trenches.

A development to have far-reaching consequences for the future occurred in 1879 when electric traction was first used in a practical fashion. Werner von Siemens formed a company and ran a public service at the Berlin Exhibition of that year. The first main line application of electrical power though was a joint electrification project by Bavaria and Austria on the line from Innsbruck to Garmisch Partenkirchen. The current used was 15,000 Volts, 16.67 herz AC, supplied from overhead wires, which was then adopted as standard.

Up to 1914 the state systems grew by both new construction and absorption of private railways, but the fortunes of the railways were changed after the First World War. The map was re-drawn and much territory was lost, particularly with the formation of Poland and the return of Alsace-Lorraine to France. Naturally locomotives and rolling stock were lost with the territory, but more still were lost through reparations, especially newish locomotives built to standard K.P.E.V. designs. Of course the least serviceable locomotives were the ones that remained behind, and new engines were badly needed, but reparations dealt a double blow as factory capacity was tied up building new locos to be sent abroad.

There were about 34,000 miles of railway in Germany when in 1920 the DR, Deutsche Reichsbahn, was formed from existing state systems and the absorption of private railways. A standardisation program was introduced for building new locomotives, adopting the Bavarian S3/6 Pacifics and various Prussian designs already in existence in significant numbers. A locomotive committee was set up to oversee a programme of development of new more modern standard types, the chairman of which was the eminent Dr. R.P. Wagner, who was thus effectively the DR's Chief Mechanical Engineer.

The principal new classes introduced were:

1925: 01 4-6-2 Pacific, 02 compound variant, (later reb. to 01)
1926: 43 2-10-0, (oil-fired) followed by the class 44 (coal-fired)
1930: 03 4-6-2 light Pacific and 41 2-8-2
1927: 24 2-6-0 light mixed traffic
1928: 64 2-6-2T a tank version of the class 24, 86 2-8-2T
1938: 50 2-10-0 universal freight loco

The DR suffered badly in depression of 1923 and in 1924 was reformed into a state-owned corporation, the Deutsche Reichsbahn-Gesellschaft (DRG), over which state took full control from 1937 onwards.

From the time of formation of the DR up to and into the Second World War was a period of consolidation, experimentation, and development. High speed trains such as the 'Flying Hamburger' diesel multiple unit were introduced, and the DRG was running some of the World's fastest steam locomotives. Indeed the World steam speed record was captured by 4-6-4 05.003, travelling at 200.4 kph on 11th May 1936, and was retained until taken by 'Mallard' the following year. Electrification was also developed in this era, mainly on lines in the south of the country, centred on Munich.

More sinister events were also taking place for political reasons, such as the confiscation of the rolling stock of the International Sleeping Car Company to form the equivalent 'Mitropa' service. After the 'Anschluss' with Austria the BBÖ's locomotives were renumbered into DR stock as Austrian railways were assimilated, then in 1938 came the invasion of Czechoslovakia, resulting in a further increase in the size of the DR, followed by Poland and the Second World War.

Locomotive factories not only in Germany, but also in the new satellite territories were turned over to production of wartime economy versions of the standard freight locos. These were the class 42 austerity equivalent of the class 44, and class 52 equivalent of the class 50. Historically, production of the class 52 was exceeded in quantity only by the Russian engineer Luposhinski's class E 0-10-0, and has been extensively documented elsewhere.

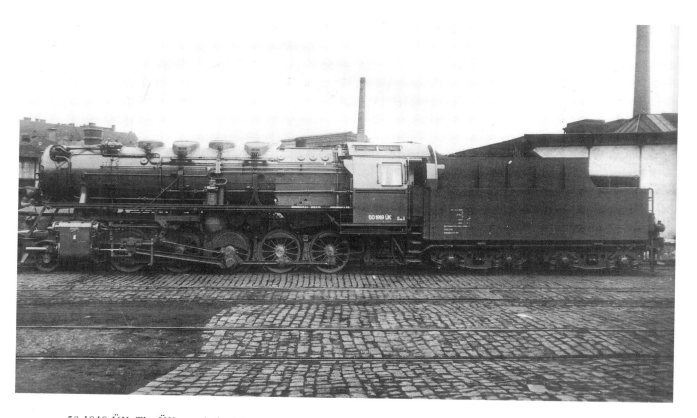

50.1919 ÜK. The ÜK stands for 'übergangs-kriegslokomotiv', transitional war locomotive, a stage between the standard class 50 2-10-0 and the wartime austerity class 52 'Kriegslok'. Photo: Č.M.S.

A comparison of the DR and DB 2-8-4T locomotives developed after 1945. If re-unification had occurred when both of these types were still active, they would have formed classes 65 and 65[1], preventing a clash of loco numbers.

65.1088-7 is one of the DR locomotives built from 1955 onwards, seen here awaiting departure from Gera hbf with the 14:15 to Altenburg on 30th December 1977.

Photo: Keith R. Chester.

65.018 represents the DB locos built 1951-56. This particular example is preserved in private ownership in Holland, and is seen approaching Dordrecht with a special on 25th May 1986, at which time the DR 2-8-4Ts were still in normal service.
Photo: Paul Cotterell.

At it's peak the DR controlled the greater part of Europe's railways, from France's Atlantic seaboard to western Russia, and from the north of Scandinavia to Greece. With such a huge territory to cover, a grand trunk railway system was planned on a massive scale to a gauge of 3000 mm. Progress reached the extent of making detailed designs for locomotives, rolling stock and stations and building wooden mock-ups of bogies.

By the end of the Second World War the railways of greater Germany had suffered extensive destruction. Over 3,700 bridges were out, nearly two-thirds of the remaining locomotive and coaching stock was unserviceable, and a quarter of the goods wagons likewise. The railway system was severed by the separation of Germany into Soviet and Western-occupied zones, and the loss of Eastern Prussia to the USSR. The splitting up of the network changed the geographical nature of the system in Western Germany. Having been a web of lines radiating from Berlin, the new emphasis was on north-south communication along the Rhine, with connections to principal regional centres which formed Bundesbahn 'Direktions'.

In East Germany, (the D.D.R.), the picture did not change so radically, but the arms of the network were of course cut back, effectively becoming international connections. Minor and secondary lines crossing the new borders became branch lines with termini at former through stations. East Germany's railways remained as the Deutsche Reichsbahn, but in West Germany control was handed back to the German people and the Deutsche Bundesbahn was formed in 1949. By this time much of the former system was working once more.

With the separation of the railways into two administrations, locomotive development took different routes in the two halves of the country. East Germany's DR did a certain amount of rebuilding, particularly the reconstruction of ex-K.P.E.V. G.12 2-10-0s, but also embarked on creating some new designs, such as the classes 65 and 83 2-8-4T, and the class 25 2-8-0.

On the DB the emphasis was mainly on rebuilding existing locomotives, although there were some new tank locos, none of which outlasted earlier K.P.E.V. types. More significant was a series of modern 2-6-2s, the class 23s, built up till 1959. The class 01s and 03s were rebuilt larger boilers and the 01^{10} Pacifics were rebuilt into class 012 (oil-fired) and 011 (coal-fired), losing their streamline casing in the process. The class 50 resumed production, numerically over-running the class series, so that locos apparently numbered in classes 51 to 53 were actually type 50s.

The DR received numerous diesel locomotives from Russian works, particularly the class 130 and variants, and the class 120 'Taiga Trommel', usually translated as 'Tiger Drums', a nickname combining the name of the Russian river Taiga and the sound they make! East Germany electrified some principal routes, though not to the extent of West Germany, and with the

notable exception of some short sections in and near Berlin. Nevertheless steam traction continued to be used in diminishing quantities until re-unification, and remains in service on some narrow-gauge systems.

In Western Germany diesel developments took the form of the 'Kleinlok', a small loco for light shunting and station pilot duties, the diesel railcar, and the diesel-hydraulic. During the 1950s and 1960s wealth and car ownership started to rise and local railways found themselves with a battle on their hands. Private and state railways were affected alike, and many lines closed or went over to the use of railcars to stay alive - a similar state of affairs to the railways in the Czech Republic and Poland today.

On the main line the V200 design was proving a success, and largely shaped the British Railways 'Western Warship' class, but hydraulic transmission, although simple in theory was in practice complicated and not always reliable. More of a success was made of the hydraulic type than in Britain, but nevertheless, modern diesels in Germany have been designed with electrical transmission.

For the steam fan the significance of the electrification programme was greater, as diesels were not a stop-gap measure produced in large quantities to get rid of steam traction, whereas that would be the longer term side effect of energising the main lines. It was decided to retain steam until electrification was complete on certain routes, which meant the target for the end of DB working steam was originally 1972, although this slipped back to 1977.

Some branch lines in the Black Forest were worked by ex-Prussian class 38s and a solitary class 78 until quite late in steam's day, and the newer class 23s and 50s were active till near

B-B V160.001, the prototype for one of the most successful diesel classes. Testing of the early examples took place in the Hamburg area in 1960, and the series production models of the class with a re-designed front end are still active, nowadays numbered in the 216 series.
Photo: DB, c/o Paul Cotterell.

the end in the Saarland. The real swansong though came with the rostering of expresses behind the 01s based at Hof and the 012s running at electric timings on the Rheine-Emden line. These workings lasted until 1974, and the use of 2-10-0s and 2-8-2s on heavy freight duties continued for another three years, the official end of steam being marked on 11th September 1977.

With the re-unification of Germany the DB and DR were merged into the DB AG - with active standard gauge steam locos still in the DR fleet. These have since been retired, but giving a new source of engines for steam preservation. Indeed steam development continues, spurred on by the environmental pressure groups, as a locomotive from the preserved EFZ line (52.8055) is at the time of writing being rebuilt in Switzerland by SLM. A technical upgrade is being given along the lines of SLMs own recent new locomotives, to include new combustion and draughting arrangements which will reduce or eliminate smoke production and improve steaming qualities and economy. Steam preservation in Germany looks not only to the past, but the future.

Preservation and electrification: 38.205, a former Saxon State Railways class XII H2 4-6-0, storms under the wires with a Berlin - Sczeczin (PKP) special, passing a DR class 243 Bo-Bo electric at Angermünde on 17th April 1995. Photo: Joachim Stübben.

Narrow Gauge in the North Sea: The Wangerooge Island Railway

by Wolfgang Ewers
All photographs by the author

103-year old 'Franzburg' and its coaches (almost a century younger!) are waiting for passengers from the mainland before departing from Wangerooge Western Pier during the centennial month of July 1997.

Deutsche Bahn AG (DB AG), successor to both Reichsbahn and Bundesbahn, is well known for its narrow gauge steam railways in the former East Germany. But how many visitors to the Saxon 750 mm gauge lines know that DB AG still runs a narrow gauge route in West Germany? The tracks on the Frisian island of Wangerooge may lack articulated Meyers and wooden planked coaches, but nevertheless they still have a charm all of their own.

At the turn of the Century, the Frisian Islands in the North Sea became some of Germany's most popular holiday resorts, however, the East Frisian Islands - between the Ems and Elbe estuaries - were ill equipped for mass tourism because they had no deep water harbours. Steamers from ports such as Harle on the North German coast had to drop anchor some distance from the shore while their passengers finished their sea voyage in small boats.

As tourist numbers increased, piers - linked by railways to the village inland - became the logical solution to this problem and were subsequently built on all East Frisian Islands except Norderney. Owned mostly by either shipping companies that served the islands or by island communities themselves, these Frisian railways varied in gauge from 600 to 1,000 mm and were either steam worked from inception or converted from horse haulage as traffic increased. In the case of Spiekeroog the railway was converted from horse haulage to diesel traction without ever using a steam locomotive. Its horse tramway was completed as early as 1885, while Borkum received its steam railway in 1888, ten years before a similar enterprise began on Juist. In contrast, the horse tramway on Langeoog did not open until 1901 - but the first train ran on Wangerooge a century ago in 1897.

The small island of Baltrum also had a freight-only 600 mm gauge line while the standard gauge (1,435 mm) network on Norderney was exclusively for military use. Indeed, the strategically important Frisian Islands were heavily fortified during both World Wars with the construction of barracks, bunkers, airfields and gun emplacements. As a result, the military not only built new lines (often exceeding the length of existing civilian track) but brought their own locomotives and rolling stock to the islands. Many of these vehicles were to remain in the peace that followed.

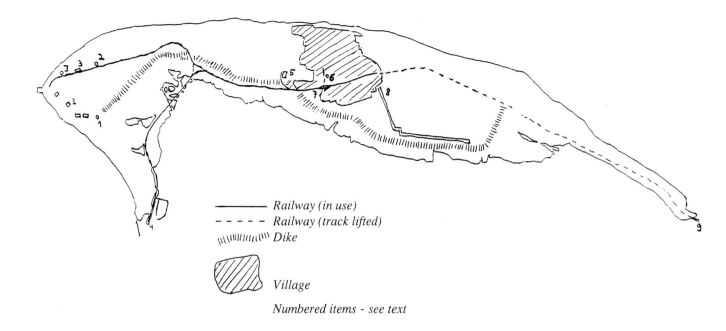

_____ Railway (in use)

- - - - - Railway (track lifted)

ιιιΙΙΙΙιιιΙΙΙΙιιΙΙΙΙΙΙΙ Dike

Village

Numbered items - see text

A Century of Struggle: The Wangerooge Island Railway from 1897 to 1997

In contrast to the neighbouring islands, Wangerooge's metre gauge railway was neither built by a shipping company nor by the islanders themselves. It was part of the Grossherzoglich Oldenburgische Eisenbahn (Grand Duchy of Oldenburg Railway, or GOE) from the beginning, and formed a logical extension of the GOE mainland line from Oldenburg to Harle by way of Jever - the latter section having been acquired from private ownership just before the official opening of the Wangerooge line on 3 July 1897.

Initially , the metre gauge metals ran almost two miles from a pier at the South Western end of the four and a half square mile island to the village in the middle. Here the railway's Eastern terminus lay in the main street and boasted a shed for its three carriages and sole locomotive.

Half way between pier and village lay Haltepunkt Saline (Saltern Halt), which was to become the first railway junction on Wangerooge in 1900 when the Navy opened a mile and a quarter long branch line to serve the Westernmost part of the island. Then, in 1904, the shipping lines which served Wangerooge from Bremerhaven and Wilhelmshaven had a pier built on the island's Eastern extremity. Another metre gauge line was built to connect this with the village, and at the same time the terminus in the main street was abandoned in favour of a new GOE station just outside the village. The new station and associated locomotive and rolling stock depot was completed in 1905 and form the basis of the buildings still in use today.

The addition of these new lines and the construction work carried out by the military prior to the First World War prompted the arrival of extra four wheeled balcony-ended carriages and four more steam locomotives between 1904 and

1913. Like their predecessor, these engines were tiny 0-4-0Ts, although a move was made toward bogie carriages after 1910.

After the Great War however, economic depression and the demilitarisation of Wangerooge caused a downturn in traffic volumes and two of the locomotives acquired for the island were sold for scrap. Then, in 1923, GOE was incorporated into the newly founded Deutsche Reichsbann Gesellschaft (DRG) after which a gradual increase in traffic led to new compartment bogie carriages totally supplanting their predecessors. A new six coupled locomotive - numbered 99 211 - also arrived in 1927, although this was a typical contractor's engine built in large numbers for industrial use rather than a DRG 'Standard' design. Either way, the locomotive shed was enlarged with two more roads in the early 1930s and has remained virtually unaltered since then.

The outbreak of the Second World War in 1939, however, ended these prosperous years and the little line once more reverted to military control. The first victims of the conflict were the two oldest 0-4-0Ts - 99 021 and 99 022 - which were despatched to the Russian Front in 1942 and never returned to the island; by which time Wangerooge had been converted into an unsinkable battleship by the so called 'Organisation Todt' (OT; a special force within the army which was involved in construction works, e.g. the building of the 'Atlantik Wall' in France and on the Channel Islands). As large quantities of building material, troops and ammunition had to be moved along the narrow gauge line 99 081, an 0-6-0T tramway locomotive, was brought in from the Palatinate. This was joined later in the War by three other steam engines, two of which arrived from Holland and the third from France, although only two of this trio actually saw service.

The station building, carriage shed and engine shed photographed from the old lighthouse on September 25th, 1996.

As the only surviving steam locomotive of Wangerooge, 99 211 (Henschel 21443/1927) has been put on display in front of the old lighthouse only a few yards from the station.

On 25 April 1945 2,300 tons of bombs fell on Wangerooge during an Allied air raid which caused many civilian casualties and damaged most of the buildings. The station building and shed, like the some of the locomotives, were hit but could be repaired although some rolling stock was destroyed.

Altogether ten steam locomotives, four diesel locomotives and a railcar were used by the military authorities on Wangerooge during the Second World War and when hostilities ceased the railcar and one of the diesel locomotives were sold to the neighbouring island of Spiekeroog. Then, in 1945 and 1949, the French locomotive and one of the Dutch ones also left Wangerooge to become Deutsche Bundesbahn (DB) Numbers 99 291 and 99 281. However both the 0-4-0T from Holland - later numbered 99 271, and the ex-Palatinate tramway engine - 99 081, remained on the island along with 99 023 and 99 211 until the first post-war diesel locomotive arrived on Wangerooge in 1952.

Numbered V11 901, this 0-6-0 diesel hydraulic was built by Messrs. Gmeinder of Mosbach and based on a 1938 design developed for 600 and 750 mm gauge Heeresfeldbahnen (the

German Army light railways). More than 300 of this type, officially designated 'HF 130C', were built up to 1943 and required little modification for use on metre gauge railways.

Within a month of V11 901 being delivered 99 081 and 99 271 had been withdrawn and scrapped soon after. When V11 902 and V11 903 arrived in 1957 - complete with more spacious cabs that offered the footplate crew better visibility - 99 211 was withdrawn and held in reserve until 1960. Fortunately it escaped the scrapper's torch to be plinthed in front of the old lighthouse near the station. This had been the last and most modern steam locomotive to run on Wangerooge, although 99 023 - the last survivor from GOE days - was officially withdrawn and scrapped in 1958.

The modernisation of the locomotive fleet was accompanied by the renewal of coaching stock. Seven steel-bodied coaches were built for the railway in 1959 using underframes from older vehicles and when DB suspended passenger services on the 750 mm Mosbach to Mudau line in 1973 five similar coaches were re-gauged for use on Wangerooge. Then, as passenger numbers increased, four additional carriages were purchased from the railway on Spiekeroog when it closed in 1981. Also from Spiekeroog came a railcar built by Waggonfabrik Wismar in 1933, while another diesel locomotive, an 0-4-0 hydraulic built by Maschinenfabrik Deutz (KHD), had arrived from the island of Juist in 1971.

A more radical change to the railways of Wangerooge however came in 1958 when boats stopped using the Eastern pier. This had often been damaged by storms, heavy seas and drifting sand, and two years later the line to it from the village had been

dismantled. In the mid 1970s the station building and goods depot were enlarged to their present form and in 1988 a private siding was built between their location and Saltern Halt to serve a new refuse transfer plant.

In the 1980s and early 1990s, Wangerooge's railways offered a colourful picture with a great variety of coaches (and a few dozen low sided and flat wagons as well) hauled by quartet of diesels. To reduce costs and simplify maintenance DB decided to standardise on two types of coaches. Fourteen new carriages, officially designated as rebuilds, were delivered from DB AG's Perleberg works. Twelve of these are standard passenger types with open platforms at each end while two are composite luggage vans, specially equipped with ramps for use with prams and wheelchairs. During normal operations, ten of these light blue and white liveried vehicles form two rakes consisting of five standard passenger coaches and one composite, with two standard passenger types being held in reserve.

Together with the coaches, two almost new locomotives arrived from the mainland. Ten 750 mm gauge diesels had been ordered by the VEB Kombinat Wilhelm Pieck (now Mansfeld Transport GmbH) prior to German reunification but with the decline of the East German economy after the collapse of the Democratic Republic of Germany they were never used. Two of these 0-6-0 hydraulics - built in Romania by the 23rd August Works at Bucharest - were then acquired by DB and refurbished and regauged for use on Wangerooge: their arrival, bearing the island's traditional red locomotive paintwork, allowed the ex-Spiekeroog railcar to be displaced to a preserved line on the mainland (via DB AG's Perleberg Works).

The first of the diesels acquired by the DB to arrive on the island was V11 901, now numbered 399 101-5. On 25th September 1996 the engine is pulling into the station with a rake of low sided wagons loaded with sand for a local building contractor.

Although its external appearance differs considerably from its sister diesel five years older, 399 102-3 is mechanically identical to 399 101-5. (September 1996).

Containers holding the passengers' luggage are being hoisted from the MS Wangerooge onto open flat wagons behind 399 102-3.

The Scene Today

Wangerooge remains a tidal harbour and boats are scheduled to sail from it to Harle accordingly - with up to four departures each day in the high season dropping to just one or two in the winter. In addition, day trips to Heligoland or to the neighbouring islands are run at infrequent intervals.

These irregular sailings from Harle are a lifeline to the island community, bringing food and beverages stowed in small containers and building material on pallets. And as there are no cars, taxis, lorries or other motor vehicles on Wangerooge, everything must go inland by rail! Whenever a boat arrives at the harbour it is met by either one or two trains. The passengers' luggage, which has also been packed in special containers, is unloaded from the vessel by a deck mounted crane on to waiting flat wagons, and as this transfer takes some time it is common for a passenger train to leave the pier first while the 'goods' follows after - often only a few hundred yards behind!

399 104-9 was named 'Heinrich' when running over the tracks of the Juist Island Railway. The locomotive was leased from Juist in 1971 and purchased for Wangerooge a year later. It is a unique engine on the island, being the only Deutz-built engine and also the only two-coupled engine amidst a horde of 0-6-0 DHs.

Until early autumn, the Youth Hostel and several school camps in the Westernmost part of the island are served with special trains which, until a few years ago, could run directly from the pier. Today, trains for the west have to run to the village before being propelled out again - a duty to which the ex-Spiekeroog railcar was often allocated in winter.

Island refuse, meanwhile, is collected by road trailer pulled by small battery vehicles and taken to the refuse transfer plant for sorting into different open settling tanks. These are then loaded onto flat wagons and hauled to the pier on an 'as required' basis to connect with a converted ex-Navy landing ship which will take the refuse ashore. Indeed, this is the same ship that carries the island's rolling stock 'as required'!

Once the passengers - numbering in their hundreds from a full ship - have been reunited with their luggage at the village station they are free to look around. Usually the doors of the engine and carriage shed are open and it is easy to watch rolling stock being repaired. The shed is well equipped and handles all such maintenance apart from wagon underframes and bodies, which are usually repaired on the mainland. They arrive back on Wangerooge aboard flat wagons, first for painting and then setting onto bogies once again. As these underframes receive the pair of bogies which has just become available, minor adjustments are usually required, standardisation still being an elusive concept on the island!

Rolling stock currently consists of fourteen coaches (all 'rebuilds' from 1992/93), and approximately fifty wagons. The latter are low sided and flat wagons, mostly bogie types, plus four tank wagons for the conveyance of fuel, two of which are privately owned. Two closed vans have been stored out of use for some time. Passenger trains usually consist of six coaches

painted in a light blue and cream livery, offering 373 seats altogether. The livery carried on the diesels is a dark red with black below the running plate.

Crews often complain about the Romanian diesels which are said to be rather unreliable, and in September 1996 both were unserviceable - with local people desperately trying to obtain spares for them! As a consequence the old Gmeinder diesels are still held in high regard for 'mainline' trains, with the Deutz doing the shunting.

In 1995 the 'Schiffsdienst und Inselbahn Wangerooge' (SIW), as the shipping company and railway are officially known, carried almost 400,000 passengers and more than 14,000 tons of freight. Since 1965 the number of passengers carried has almost doubled and the future looks bright for the island's system, either being retained by DB AG or privatised (as happened to Rugen's 750 mm line).

1997 - The Jubilee Year

In July 1997 Wangerooge celebrated the Centennial of its railway. With no intention to restore 99 211 to working order, an engine from the 'Deutscher Eisenbahn-Verein' (DEV) at Bruch hausen-Vilsen (south of Bremen) was hired. On 1st July 1997 'Franzburg', an 0-4-0T built in 1894 by Stettiner Maschinenbau-Aktiengesellschaft Vulkan in Stettin for the Franzburger Kreisbahnen, arrived on the island, being transported by the ex-landing ship 'Harlestrand'. This engine strongly resembles the first locomotives acquired by the GOE, with its small boiler and side tanks, and large stovepipe chimney. Until the end of July 'Franzburg' hauled a number of trains between pier and village, not only during the jubilee weekend of July 26/27th, but also before and after this event. During these weekends those who paid the modest fare of five Deutsche Mark could also enjoy a 'railtour' over the whole island with photo stops at the new lighthouse and within the bird sanctuary (where the author's own attempts ended in disaster following an interrogation by an ambitious park ranger)!

Those who wish to pay a visit to the island or even want to spend a holiday on Wangerooge may write to: Nordseeheilbad Wangerooge, Postfach 220, D-26476 Wangerooge. Both the islanders and the DB AG staff are very friendly people and they will pass on every kind of information a railfan requires. For a look into the shed please contact the ticket and information office beforehand. The island museum which is situated inside the old lighthouse has an interesting collection of old photographs and postcards of the railway. Currently there is only one small brochure available exclusively on the Wangerooge railway. It is titled '100 Jahre Inselbahn Wangerooge', and can be obtained from the ticket offices at both Wangerooge and Harle. The book "Die Nordsee-Inselbahnen" by Hans Wolfgang Rogl (Alba Publikation Düsseldorf, 6th edition 1996) is highly recommended for excellent information on all the railways of the Frisian Islands, past and present.

On 19th July 1997 at the village station, DEV loco 'Franzburg' runs round a train just brought in from the harbour as 399 105-6, the first of the Romanian diesels, attends to freight traffic.

0-4-0T 'Franzburg' was not only used on passenger trains during the jubilee month, but also goods. The train shown is being loaded from the MS Wangerooge berthed at the Western Pier on 19th July 1997.

Bibliography:

Die Nordsee-Inselbahnen by Hans Wolfgang Rogl, Alba Publikation, Düsseldorf, 4th edition 1990

Archiv deutscher Klein- und Privatbahnen: Niedersachsen by Hans Wolfgang Rogl. Transpress Verlag, Stuttgart, 1996

Deutsche Klein- und Privatbahnen, Teil 2: Niedersachsen by Gerd Wolff. Verlag Wolfgang Zeunert, Gifhorn, 1973

Die Privatbahnen in der Bundesrepublik Deutschland by Gerd Wolff. Eisenbahn-Kurier Verlag, Freiburg, 1984

100 Jahre Inselbahn Wangerooge by Peter Löffler (editor), issued by DB AG, Harlesiel, 1997

Dampflok-Archiv 4: Baureihen 97, 98 und 99 by Manfred Weisbrod and Wolfgang Petznick. Transpress, 2nd edition 1983

Taschenbuch Deutsche Schmalspur-Dampflokomotiven by Horst J. Obermayer. Franckh'sche Verlagshandlung, Stuttgart, 3rd edition 1977

Taschenbuch Deutsche Diesellokomotiven by Horst J. Obermayer. Franckh'sche Verlagshandlung, Stuttgart, 1st edition 1972

Eisenbahn-Fahrzeug-Katalog, Band 2: Deutsche Bundesbahn by Axel Enderlein. GeraNova Zeitschriftenverlag, Munchen 1993

Eisenbahn-Fahrzeug-Katalog, Band 3: Wagen by Dr. Martin Pabst. GeraNova Zeitschriftenverlag, Munchen 1994

Deutsche Bahnbetriebswerke (loose leaf series) by Matthias Fuhrmann. GeraNova Zeitschriftenverlag, Munchen 1994

Acknowledgement:

Thanks go to Alan Drewett for his help in proofreading and his editorial assistance.

Appendix 1: Steam Locomotives

GOE No.	DRG/DB No.	Wheels	Builder	Works No./Year	Notes
1	---	0-4-0 T	Märkische Lokfabrik	148/1896	1897-ca.1920, bought new, scrapped ca. 1920
2	---	0-4-0 T	Maschinenbau-Gesellschaft Heilbronn	358/1898	1904-ca.1920, bought second hand (previous name „Neckar"), scrapped ca. 1920
3	99 021	0-4-0 T	Freudenstein & Co.	194/1904	1910-1942, bought second hand, to Russian Front in 1942
4	99 022	0-4-0 T	Hanomag	5876/1910	1910-1942, bought new, to Russian Front in 1942
5	99 023	0-4-0 T	Hanomag	6930/1913	1913-1957, bought new, scrapped in 1958
---	99 211	0-6-0 T	Henschel & Sohn	21443/1927	1927-1958, bought new, nicknamed 'Klara', held in reserve until 1960, put on display in 1968
---	99 081	0-6-0 T tramway locomotive	Krauss & Co.	2082/1889	1939-1952, transferred from the Palatinate (ex class L 1 „Dannstadt"), scrapped in 1953
---	99 271 (number applied after WWII)	0-4-0 T	Jung	2483/1918	1944-1952, requisitioned by OT, ex Zeenwsch-Vlaamsche Tramweg Maatschappij No. 21, scrapped in 1953
---	(99 281) (number applied upon return to the mainland)	0-6-0 T	Weidknecht	165/1910	(1944) requisitioned by OT in France, never used on the island, to mainland in 1945
---	99 291 (number applied after WWII)	0-6-0 T	Orenstein & Koppel	4801/1911	1944-1949, requisitioned by OT from an unknown line (contractor?), to mainland in 1949
---	---	0-4-0 T	Vulcan (Stettin)	1363/1894	07/1997, built for Franzburger Kreisbahnen, became DR No. 99 5605 in 1949, withdrawn in 1969, to Freizeitpark Minidom in 1973, to DEV in 1980, named 'Franzburg'

Appendix 2: Diesel Locomotives and Railcars

pre-1968 DB Nos.	1968-1992 DB No./ current DB AG No.	Type/ Horsepower	Builder	Works No./ Year	Notes
V11 901 Köf 99 501	329 501/ 399 101	0-6-0 DH/ 130 hp	Gmeinder	4378/1952	acquired new in 1952, narrow cab
V11 902 Köf 99 502	329 501/ 399 102	0-6-0 DH/ 130 hp	Gmeinder	5038/1957	acquired new in 1957, wide cab
V11 903 Köf 99 503	329 503/ 399 103	0-6-0 DH/ 130 hp	Gmeinder	5039/1957	acquired new in 1957, wide cab
---	329 504/ 399 104	0-4-0 DH/ 120 hp	Klöckner-Humboldt-Deutz (KHD)	46841/1952	ex Inselbahn Juist „Heinrich", leased 1971/72, bought in 1972
---	---/ 399 105	0-6-0 DH/ 245 hp	23 August Locomotive Works (Model L 18 H-C)	?/1990	ex Mansfeld Transport GmbH, bought and rebuilt in 1992/93, in service since Summer 1993
---	---/ 399 106	0-6-0 DH/ 245 hp	23 August Locomotive Works (Model L 18 H-C)	?/1990	ex Mansfeld Transport GmbH, bought and rebuilt in 1992/93, in service since Summer 1993
---	699 001/ 399 001 (renumbered prior to 1992)	B-B railcar/ 106 hp	Waggonfabrik Wismar	20220/1933	ex Kreisbahn Emden-Pewsum-Greetsiel VT 61, ex Inselbahn Spiekeroog VT 5, acquired in 1981, left the island in 1993

NB:

- All engines are painted in dark red.
- 'Inselbahn' means island railway; 'Kreisbahn' or 'Kleinbahn' are independent light railways.
- In September 1996 both Romanian diesels were stored unserviceable. In July 1997 at least one engine was observed in regular service.
- The railcar was first brought to Perleberg Works (a division of Wittenberge Works). In 1995 it has been sold to DEV (Deutscher Eisenbahn-Verein) at Bruchhausen-Vilsen for use on their preserved line to Asendorf. Being in rather poor condition it has not yet been restored to working order.
- Over the years further small railcars for inspection purposes have been in use.

II. Rolling Stock

Currently there are fourteen coaches (all „rebuilds" from 1992/93) and approx. 50 wagons on the island. The latter consist of low sided wagons and flat wagons (most of them bogie types) plus four tank wagons for the conveyance of fuel (two which are privately owned). Two closed vans are sitting on the scrap track. Passenger trains usually consist of six coaches offering 373 seats altogether. Coaches are painted light blue and cream. For the jubilee weekend 'Franzburg' was running with a DEV 'support coach' (actually a closed four-wheel van) and a four-wheel baggage car (restored to running order and repainted for the event). One of the 1959 built coaches can be seen plinthed in front of the former station building at Harlesiel on the mainland.

Coals From Alsdorf

by D. Trevor Rowe and Paul Cotterell

There were not many places where working steam could be found in West Germany by 1989, even at industrial sites, but one such was well known and easily accessible, being conveniently situated near the Dutch and Belgian borders near a point where the E40 and E314 motorways converge just beyond Aachen. Slightly to the north is the town of Alsdorf, unremarkable except for the Grube Anna colliery located within a few minutes walk of the town centre right alongside the DB (goods only) station.

The Eschweiler Bergwerks Verein (EBV) have a number of collieries in the area, but steam activity was finally concentrated at Alsdorf. Fortunately, only the DB tracks separate the public from those of the colliery, and there was a nearby level crossing, so photography could be carried out without any problem, even with a standard lens.

Up to 1983 there were a dozen steam locomotives at Grube Anna, all 0-8-0Ts or 0-6-0Ts, of pre- and post-war construction, and the majority from Krupp and Henschel. After that date a decline set in and many of the locos were scrapped or sold for preservation. One one visit as late as 1988 four 0-8-0Ts were active, and one of them, No. 3 (Henschel 1949), was seen working in June 1989, indeed steam may have continued to work on a limited scale just into the 1990s.

Naturally, a mine producing enough coal to keep this many industrial locos busy was generating heavy traffic for the DB to work forward. Class 50 2-10-0s were used single and double-heading to haul the trains of hopper wagons once on Bundesbahn metals, and Paul Cotterell found them in abundance on his visits to Alsdorf in the autumns of 1972/73.

EBV locos from two different eras working in the grimy atmosphere of Alsdorf in January 1986.
Anna N.2 was built in 1946 (Henschel 29884), and Anna 10 in 1930 (BMAG 9963). Photo: D. Trevor Rowe.

The line out from the colliery to the exchange sidings was uphill, so when there was a loaded train to be moved the EBV tanks could be seen working at their hardest. The top photo shows No. 4 running bunker first, with No. 5 caught in the lower shot. Both of them are Henschel 0-8-0Ts. Photos: Paul Cotterell, 25th September 1972.

Upper: Anna N.2 blasts forth with a rake of hoppers on a wintery day in January 1986. Photo: D. Trevor Rowe.
Lower: Alsdorf line-up - DB class 50 2-10-0s and EBV Henschel 0-8-0Ts on 22nd October 1973. Photo Paul Cotterell.

Double-headed 2-10-0s lift an early evening load of coal away from the Grube Anna mine in October 1973. Photos: Paul Cotterell.

STEAM WHERE I GREW UP

by Joachim Stübben
All photographs by the author

Gremberg shed in 1967, with 41 178 from Köln-Eifeltor and the depot's own 55 4141.

Thirty Years Ago: The Retreat of Prussian Steam

I grew up in Krefeld, an industrial town near Düsseldorf. In the industry belt between Aachen and Dortmund Prussian locomotives still held a relatively strong position at the beginning of the second half of the sixties (when I started photographing locomotives). Classes 55.25 and 94.5 were still numerous, but there were also the last surviving specimens of classes 38.10, 56.2, 57.10, 78.0 and 93.5 still doing their duty or at least serviceable. But it was clear that they would soon have to give way to diesels.

In 1964, as an eleven year old boy, I started to build up my own collection of pictures of steam locomotives. In the first years my photographic activity was, unfortunately, confined to taking pictures at the platform, in the shed or on the scrapyard. It was not before 1968 that I started waiting for steam out on the open track, inspired by the desire to catch more of the beauty and dynamics of steam power with the camera. When I was fourteen years old I said ambitiously to myself that I would strive to equal the rail photographers Jean-Michel Hartmann and Ludwig Rotthowe.

When I was a child my conception of the world of trains was shaped by Karl-Ernst Maedel's five or six books, among which the autobiographical book "Bekenntnisse eines Eisenbahnnarren" (Confessions of A Rail Enthusiast) had an especially powerful influence on me. This book contains among other remarkable things the unforgettable chapter "Narrenromanze" (A Fool's Brief Love Affair), which I summarize here in few words:

In the 1930s the narrator (the author as a young man) meets a pretty young actress on an express train to Frankfurt/M. The conversation proceeds in a very promising way, but when the train pulls into Frankfurt Hbf (main station) the narrator is spellbound by the unexpected sight of Germany's most powerful express steam loco, the 4-8-4 streamlined 06 class (of which only two examples were built) on a track at the far end of the station hall. He leaves the young lady alone on the platform, rushes away to get near the 06, then suddenly comes back to his senses, hastens back to the place where he had left the lady, but she has gone and the narrator says to himself: "What a stupid blind fool am I"

I must have read this episode at the age of twelve, (children used to read books in those days and there was no TV in my parents' home at that time!), and I considered it a warning and decided that I would never forget the message.

In the industrial zone from Aachen to Dortmund the following sheds had steam engines in 1967: Aachen, Dortmund-Rbf, Duisburg-Wedau, Gelsenkirchen-Bismarck, Gremberg, Hagen-Gbf, Hohenbudberg, Köln-Deutzerfeld, Köln-Eifeltor, Mönchengladbach, Neuss, Oberhausen-Osterfeld, Rheydt, Stolberg, Wanne-Eickel, Wuppertal-Vohwinkel.

In the 1960s my father and I usually planned our trips without knowing exactly what we could expect in the sheds we were going to visit, but somehow this uncertainty added to the pleasure and sometimes we were surprised to see a rare specimen. One particular Saturday in the year 1967 we made an excursion to the sheds Gremberg (near Porz, a few kilometres south of Cologne) and Köln-Deutzerfeld (in the centre of Cologne, at a distance of about two kilometres from its famous cathedral, but on the other side of the Rhine).

Right: Ex-K.P.E.V. class G 10 0-10-0 57 1735 at Hagen in 1967.

Below: Pacifics on shed at Köln-Deutzerfeld in 1967; 03 164, 03 268, Mönchengladbach's 03 221, and from Trier 01 061.

Above: 62 003 at Gremberg, formerly a Krefeld loco. Below: Ten-coupled locos at Wuppertal-Vohwinkel, 94 1207 and 44 948.

At Gremberg 55 4141, which was standing next to 41 178, represented the very successful Prussian 0-8-0 G 8.1 class which was used not only in the huge shunting yard, but also on local goods trains, whereas the 41 and 50 class were used on both local and through goods trains in almost all directions. 41 178 belonged to the 2-8-2 41 class, designed for fast goods trains. The home shed of these locos, however, was not Gremberg, but Köln-Eifeltor on the opposite (left) side of the Rhine. We also met some locos of the ubiquitous 50 class, which were still so numerous in those days that sometimes we were almost angry when we saw one because we preferred the more unusual locomotives.

On a siding near the Gremberg shed we saw two very rare locomotives: 62 003 represented a class of fast tank locos of which only 15 examples had been built. This loco had belonged to the depot of my home town Krefeld. Only one locomotive of this class survived (62 015) and was working tourist trains from Cologne to Kreuzberg/Ahr in autumn 1996.

On the same track as 62 003 and face to face to it stood 17 218, a Prussian express train locomotive of the S 10.2 class. The interior of its boiler lay partially open, probably because the loco had been used at the "Lokführerschule" (engine drivers' school) at Troisdorf. Unfortunately this loco was scrapped even though it was the last of its kind.

In the afternoon we travelled to the centre of Cologne to visit the Köln-Deutzerfeld shed. A fine line-up of Pacifics (01 from Trier and 03 from Mönchengladbach) was to be seen in front of the shed whereas Prussia's glory was represented only by 78 271 (4-6-4 Prussian T 18), which was preparing for departure with a passenger train, and 38 1889 (4-6-0 Prussian P 8), which stood on the other side of the shed, not under steam. Both locomotives survived for a while, not at Köln-Deutzerfeld, however: 78 271 was soon transferred to Hamburg-Altona and 38 1889 to Gremberg.

Another very "successful" 1967 excursion was the one to the sheds of Wuppertal-Vohwinkel and Hagen. In Wuppertal we saw, inside and in front of the shed, the following classes: 44, 50, 78 and 94.5 (several of these heavy 0-10-0 Prussian shunters were present). 78 159 was cold and appeared, at the end of 1967, on the list of locomotives that had definitely quit service. In the open air we also saw two 2-8-2 86 class tank engines, without number plates, which must have been the last of their kind in this area.

In the afternoon we visited Hagen. The oil-fired 03.10, a modernized three-cylinder version of the 03 class, had been withdrawn from service in 1966, but at least four of them were still to be seen on a siding a year later. None of them were saved though.

On the afternoon of our visit to Hagen in 1967 2-6-2 no. 23 042 had brought in a passenger train from Bestwig.

Retired 03¹⁰s at Hagen: 03 1008 above, showing the tender with anti-dust covers, and an unidentified example below.

23 042 had come with a passenger train from Bestwig. The 23 class was a modern 2-6-2 loco designed after the Second World War for passenger service, and 23 105 was the last steam locomotive produced for DB.

During our visit V 200 081 rumbled onto the turntable, and the picture shows the partially ruined structure of the shed roof in the background. At this time Hamm depot had 33 members of the class allocated.

In 1967, the sheds of Hagen and Haltingen had the last specimens of the 57.10 class (Prussian G 10, a 0-10-0 loco for goods trains). When I photographed them I had no idea that twenty-four years later I would get a job at the German Department of the University of Sibiu (Roumania), and would be able to watch a modernized version of the G 10 built in Roumania shunting every day! Big numbers of the G 10 class had played an important part in the darkest period of German history: Equipped with anti-freeze devices they pulled military trains in the Soviet Union and long trains of goods vans loaded with people to the extermination camps in occupied Poland.

I wish to thank my father, who died in 1987, for making these early excursions possible. When I was a child my parents would, of course, not let me travel all by myself, so my father took me by car or by train to some of the places I desired to visit, even though train photography was not his hobby, and I wish to thank my father and my mother, who died in 1994, for familiarising me with the work in the dark-room. My father used to work with the enlarger and my mother was busy with the papers in the trays with the different fluids. Nowadays very few children and teenagers learn this technique from either their parents or at school. It is on the one hand very time-consuming if best results are intended, but on the other hand very satisfying.

We railfans sometimes find it difficult to make our emotions understandable to people who do not share our enthusiasm. Therefore I was very pleased when recently a young lady, an art student, who is working on a series of etchings representing industrial buildings, trains etc., asked me to give her two of my old photographs showing steam locomotives looking out of the open doors of the sheds at Gremberg and Wuppertal, because she felt inspired by the fine ensemble of circular and straight lines, of light and shadow....

Wuppertal-Vohwinkel, 1967.

West German Narrow Gauge Steam At Work In 1953

Photographed by Ian G.T. Duncan

1) The Brohltalbahn, metre gauge.

Mallet 0-4-4-0T No. 12 shunting at Brohl on 27th July 1953. (Humbolt 1473/1919). Sister loco no. 11 has been preserved by the DGEG.

Crossing a substantial viaduct on the line, hauling a goods train is no. 2, a larger 0-6-6-0T Mallet, built by Hanomag in 1928 (works no. 10570).

A closer view of no. 2 running over dual-gauge points at the junction with the standard gauge. Bohltalbahn locos were fitted with two sets of buffers and couplings, the standard gauge set being located off-centre for shunting standard gauge wagons. The railways own metre gauge stock used the single centrally fitted buffer and coupling.

2) The Kerkerbachbahn,
   metre gauge

Kerkerbachbahn no. 4 was one of two 2-6-0s built by in 1914 for Siam (Thailand), but which were never sent due to the war, and in fact were originally supplied to the Brohltalbahn. They were Krauss 6978/9, the last pair of a larger series of Siamese locos, the latter of which is illustrated here. Both ended up on the Kerkerbachbahn, but no. 4 lasted longer than no. 3, working until 1957.

Kerkerbachbahn 2-10-2T no. 15 was built by Henschel in 1941 (works no. 26169), and is also fitted with coupling and buffing gear for working over dual gauge tracks. Photo taken in July 1953.

3) The Schussenreid system,
   750 mm gauge

*97.704 was built for the Deutsche
Reichsbahn, but is a modernised version
of the 0-10-0Ts built for railways in
Saxony. On 25th July 1953 97.704 was
working a mixed passenger and freight
train at Maselheim.*

*A neatly loaded standard-gauge wagon
is being shunted on a pair of
independent 750 mm gauge carrying
bogies at Maselheim. The narrow
gauge bogies are not connected under
the wagon, (although they are clamped
round the axles), so all tractive force is
transmitted through the wagon's own
underframe.*

4) The Rhein-Sieg Eisenbahn,
   785 mm gauge

*One of the most modern narrow
gauge locomotives was RSE no. 53,
photographed at Beul. This superheated 2-10-2T was built by Jung in
1944, (works no. 10175), and has
been saved for preservation by the
DGEG.*

5) The Gelsenkirchen Bahn

At Gelsenkirchen, near the Dutch border were seen two 0-4+4-0T compound Mallets, out of use but by appearances still operable. On the left is no. 3, and no. 4 is shown below.

The circular plates on the cabside are not legible, but the rectangular plates above read 'G.K.B. 3mm' and 'G.K.B. 4mm' respectively.

The Mansfeld Copper Railway

by Keith Chester

Mansfeld 750mm gauge 0-8-0T no. 11 shunting at the August-Bebel-Hütte, Helbra, on 11th September 1989.

Copper has been mined and smelted in the Mansfelder Land, an area bounded by the towns of Hettstedt, Eisleben, Sangerhausen and Allstedt, since the beginning of the thirteenth century. Transportation between the mines and foundries in the region and then on to the market had traditionally been by pack wagon. This slow and costly expedient meant that as Germany rapidly industrialised in the mid nineteenth century, any development of the Mansfeld copper industry was held back. The hilly terrain of the area had deterred the construction of a standard gauge railway, which was deemed too expensive, and alternatives were sought. "Road-trains", hauled by a traction engine, were unsuccessfully tried in 1866 and a ropeway system, introduced in 1871, also proved unsatisfactory. Finally the solution was found in a locomotive-operated narrow gauge railway, construction of which was authorised in 1878. The initial section, a 5.5km long 750mm gauge line from the Glückhilf shaft at Welfesholz and the foundries at Hettstedt, was opened on 15 November 1880.

By 1906 the railway was operating 29 steam locos, 705 wagons and 30 passenger coaches over a "mainline" of 48 km and a further 24 km of branches and sidings. The system continued to be expanded, both on the 750 mm gauge and with the provision of 1,435 mm gauge sidings, until the mid 1920s. Efforts were made to modernise operations from the early 1930s onwards: these included the introduction of new rolling stock, notably 20 tonne bogie hoppers, and in 1932 of four powerful superheated 0-8-0Ts, built by Orenstein & Koppel; two similar locos were acquired in 1936 and 1940. At the same time air brakes were introduced for the first time and gradually the old system of hand brakes was abandoned. Real progress, however, was hampered first by the severe slump in the German economy in the 1930s and then the outbreak of war.

After the defeat of Hitler's Germany the railway found itself in the Soviet administered zone, which duly became the German Democratic Republic in 1949. The previous year, on 1 July 1948, the copper mines and works had been nationalised and formed into the Mansfeld Kombinat; in 1951 it also acquired the name of the first president of the GDR - Wilhelm Pieck.

Great efforts were made to rebuild and upgrade the railway. New, heavier, rolling stock was obtained, as were, between 1949 and 1954, ten additional steam locos. These included the so-called "Stalinlok", an Op-2 class 0-8-0 originally built by LKM Babelsberg as a 70th birthday present for Stalin. Other new locos were two Gr type 0-8-0s and two 2-10-2Ts, basically of the same design as the K57.9 type 2-10-2Ts constructed by LKM in the early 1950s for the DR.

The railway flourished in the 1950s as never before as the GDR began the slow process of economic recovery. But even as it was carrying unprecedented levels of traffic, so its importance began to wane: passenger services were transferred to the road: a new 1,435 mm gauge siding at Helbra rendered many of the

This saturated 0-6-0T (Henschel 13788/1916) was the second loco at Mansfeld to carry the number one. The photo was taken in the 1940s and the loco, like many others on the railway, was finally scrapped in 1967.

"Patriot" (works no. LKM 32020/1953), was one of two 2-10-2Ts built by the former O&K works for the VEB Mansfeld Kombinat Wilhelm Pieck. Unlike "Patriot", sister engine "Pionier" was fitted with a feedwater heater. The DR acquired 24 similar locos, many of which can still be found running on the 750 mm gauge lines of the newly-formed Deutsche Bahn AG.

Both photos on this page: K.R. Chester collection.

Rollwagen trains previously operated over the railway superfluous. This process of decline was accelerated in the 1960s as the operations of the Kombinat were gradually modernised and rationalised; in addition many of the copper mines were worked out and closed. With the exception of the O&K 0-8-0Ts, all the steam locos had been scrapped by 1970. By the mid 1980s a few diesels and only four of the 0-8-0Ts remained in service, for shunting and working trains between the August-Bebel-Hütte at Helbra and the Kupfer-Silber-Hütte (Hettstedt).

Apart from the occasional rather vague report this all went by and large unrecorded in the English railway press. In the early summer of 1989 it began to look like I could be in the area the following September, so I wrote to the enterprise enquiring if they were still using steam and optimistically requesting permission to photograph the locos at work. Much to my surprise a reply came which not only confirmed the continued use of steam but which also included a permit to photograph the Kombinat's locos. I was to present myself at the main gate of the workshops at Klostermansfeld at 10 am on 11 September 1989.

The workshops themselves proved to be large and well-equipped, far in excess of the requirements of the railway. Since the reunification of Germany they have been privatised and today, trading under the name of MaLoWa, are one of the growing number of centres offering professional engineering services to the burgeoning European steam locomotive preservation movement. To British enthusiasts they are best known as the works which repaired the ex-LNER B12 class 4-6-0 no 61572. In the GDR of 1989, however, this was all in the future and it was disappointing to find only three cold 0-8-0Ts in the shops. On enquiring, somewhat tentatively, whether anything was in steam that day, I was told that no. 11 was shunting at the nearby August-Bebel works at Helbra.

The large copper foundry at Helbra was typically East European - polluting, over-manned and using out-dated technology. By the late 1980s even the Communists had decided that enough was enough and much of the Kombinat was slated for closure in 1990. Thus when I arrived in September activity was already at a low ebb. Whilst a loco was steamed every day it was only required to shunt the August-Bebel-Hütte and about two or three times a week to work a train to Hettstedt.

Initially I was disappointed to discover that on the day of my visit no. 11 was confined to the works and yard at Helbra, but this soon turned to my advantage. The wording of my photo permit was rather vague: it entitled me to photograph the steam locomotives of the Kombinat without specifying where and, by extension, without saying where not. Using this I was able to convince the security guards at the works that this permitted me to photograph no. 11 not only in those few areas to which there was general public access, but also inside the works. So for the next two or three hours, I followed no. 11 around as she shunted the August-Bebel works, all the time photographing quite freely.

I couldn't have left it much later for a little more than seven weeks after my visit to Helbra, on 9 November 1989, the Berlin Wall was breached and the GDR in effect ceased to exist. The August-Bebel works closed at the end of that momentous year and with it the 750 mm gauge railway which had served the copper mines and works of the Mansfelder Land for well over a century.

Over the years the Mansfeld AG and later on the Wilhelm Pieck Kombinat operated a total of thirteen standard gauge locos. "Kupferberg", pictured here in 1951, was supplied by Henschel (works number 5816?) in 1901 for the then newly opened exchange sidings at Eisleben. It was transferred in 1954 to the brass foundry situated at Hettstedt.

Photo: Keith R. Chester Collection

Top: Mansfeld Copper Railway 0-8-0T no. 11 (O&K 13216/1940) shunting standard gauge stock on transporter wagons at Helbra.

Above: How much of this scene remains today? Have the wagons, like no. 11, been preserved? Certainly the Ikarus bus waiting for the 0-8-0T to cross the main road which ran through the middle of the August-Bebel-Hutte has long disappeared, but what of the offices of the works, seen in the top left of the picture? 11 September 1989.   *Both photos: Keith R. Chester*

RHEINE - EMDEN
DB Express Steam's Last Line
Photographed by Paul Cotterell & Paul Catchpole

After British Railways steam finished in 1968, there was still plenty of activity to be found in Germany, particularly around the Hof area, where express steam finished only a short while before the Rheine - Emden locos lost their passenger turns. Rheine, however, had the advantage of being closer to the UK, within range of a weekend trip even, as it is situated only just beyond the Dutch border. Many British enthusiasts made their pilgrimage as well as German steam fans, and for many it was the first sight of 'foreign' steam.

How strange were these machines to British eyes, with pipes and apparatus outside the boiler, detail design quite unlike anything on BR, and red on everything below the running plate. The paint finish on the boilers seemed at close quarters to be akin to the bituminous underseal on my first Morris Minor! If the appearance of German locomotives was an acquired taste, the quality and quantity of steam action on this line left no room for doubt.

Left: The three-cylinder class 011 Pacifics found their last duties on the Rheine - Emden line and at Minden Testing Station. On 21st May 1969 011 093-2 stands with empty stock near one of Rheine's water cranes.   *Photo: Paul Cotterell.*

Below: 011 070-0 leaving Rheine with a Norddeich - Köln train on 18th August 1969.   *Photo: Paul Cotterell.*

Top: Oil-fired DB Pacific 012 060-0 approaches Bentlage crossing with an express from Norddeich on 21st May 1969.
Photo: Paul Cotterell.

Right: Nearly five years later, on 19th March 1974, 012 100-4 departs with a southbound passenger train from Emden. Note the side of the tender which has been repaired with a real motley collection of welded patches!
Photo: Paul Catchpole.

Pacific 012 064-2 clears its throat on departure from Rheine with a train to Norddeich on 21st May 1969. Photo: Paul Cotterell

Another passenger departure for Norddeich behind a three-cylinder Pacific, 012 068-3 seen on 19th August 1969. Photo: Paul Cotterell.

Just north of Rheine is Bentlage, where 042 052-1 was caught on film with a freight working on 19th August 1969. Photo: Paul Cotterell.

2-8-2 number 042 356-6 hammers out of Rheine with a northbound mixed freight on a rainy 20th May 1969. Photo: Paul Cotterell

Left: An unidentified class 042 2-8-2 bursts out from under the bridge near Rheine station, regulator wide open, steam streaming from the drain-cocks, and just a slight wisp escaping from the valve chest.
Photo: Paul Catchpole, 22nd March 1974.

Below: Both oil and coal-fired versions of the three-cylinder heavy freight 2-10-0 worked up to Emden and Norddeich. All had started out as class (0)44 coal burners, but some were converted to oil, and became class 043. On May 21st 1969 an unidentified 043 leaves Rheine with cars.
Photo: Paul Cotterell.

Bottom: All the class 043s had been based at Kassel and Rheine, but during 1973 the class was concentrated in its entirety at Rheine, which had none of the 044s at that time. Long-term Rheine resident 043 673-6 runs light-engine through the station in March 1974.
Photo: Paul Catchpole.

A large proportion of freight traffic consisted of trains of coal and iron ore hopper wagons running to and from Emden docks, such as this example hauled by coal-fired 2-10-0 number 044 671-6 on 21st May 1969. Photo: Paul Cotterell.

A ground-shaking combination: the distinctive beat of a three-cylinder machine followed by the roar of rumbling hoppers. This was the music played by 044 219-4. 21st May 1969. Photo: Paul Cotterell

044 682-3 disturbs the peace at Rheine with a trainload of Volkswagens - the pile of coal in the tender gives a reminder that most of these brutes had their 49 sq. ft. grate fired by hand. 20th May 1969. Photo: Paul Cotterell.

Preparing to take a freight out of Emden on 19th March 1974 are lightweight class 50 2-10-0 no. 053 188-0 and a class 43. About 750 class 50s and nearly 300 class 043/044s were still in service in Germany at this time. The class 50s were numbered in series 050 to 053 by the DB, purely due to the quantity built. There was no conflict between the 052 series and the 'Kriegslok' class 52s as the latter had been withdrawn from the DB by the time the 50s were renumbered.

In March 1974 fourteen Pacifics remained on the active list - one elusive class 011 and thirteen 012s, and when they were eventually replaced by diesels, passenger schedules were slowed down by five minutes. Some passenger turns in the area were also worked by the 042s and 050s, and these mixed traffic classes outlasted the Pacifics. By mid-1976 there were just 33 booked steam turns in Germany, all for Rheine's 043s, although a few 042s were kept on for 'as required' mixed freights. The official end of DB steam in Germany was marked by a weekend of steam activity at Rheine on 10th and 11th September 1977.

THE REKO-IVK STORY

by Dr. Günter Koch

Photographs by Dr. Günter Koch and Michael Koch

The approach into Oschatz freight yard was on a steep gradient and usually required the help of the yard engine as a pilot, but a triple-header was rare. On 20th September 1990, 99 1582-8 pilots 99 1561-2 and 99 1564-6 into the yard, but the latter was in light steam only, being transferred from Mügeln shed to Görlitz works for overhaul. All three locomotives still survive.   *Photo: Dr. G. Koch.*

Twenty-two four-cylinder compound 0-4-4-0T Meyer articulated locomotives of ex-Saxon class IVK were built new in 1962-67 by the East German Deutsche Reichsbahn (DR) for their 750 mm narrow gauge. Eight members of this class survive in working order and these are the only post-war compounds which can still be observed in steam today.

Obviously the reason why these engines are not usually looked upon as new is due to the fact that they were designated as "reconstruction" or "REKO" locomotives by the DR, which under normal circumstances would indicate that they were thoroughly rebuilt but not fundamentally new, and to strengthen this impression they were given numbers of existing locomotives. Nevertheless they were in actual fact fundamentally new engines, bearing their own identity, not related to the original Hartmann-built locos whose numbers they

bore and which were scrapped to make space for them. The answer to the question why the DR designated them "REKO" may sound unbelievable but is true: it was a camouflage to avoid some special problems inherent in former GDR state bureaucracy. "New constructions" of locomotives were to be built by the locomotive industry which was under the control of the Ministry of Heavy Machinery Construction, and hence would have required authorisation by that body, but the DR had painfully experienced that this could not be easily obtained. To avoid any more disappointments the DR decided to declare them "reconstructions" and to build them in their own repair works.

The situation on the East German narrow gauge in the mid-1950's, some ten years after the disastrous war, was desperate. The progress of rebuilding the country in general, and of railways in particular, proceeded much more slowly than in

West Germany, and narrow gauge railways were certainly not in the forefront of interest.

In this atmosphere of general neglect, lines started to be closed and dismantled, but there were enough narrow gauge branches which served important industries in regions where the general infrastructure, and especially the roads, were inadequate and where closure was out of the question. Some relief had been gained by the supply of 24 heavy 2-10-2T locomotives of 8.6 t axle load in 1952-4, built to a modified pre-war design by the former O&K factory at Babelsberg, but these were too heavy for the many lightly laid branches worked by the ageing "Saxon Meyers" of class IVK, a Hartmann design dating back to 1891, and by now badly run down. In 1955, the design of a light 2-8-2T was proposed as a replacement but was not authorised. Instead, after lengthy discussions a B'B' diesel-hydraulic locomotive was approved and two prototypes built at Babelsberg in 1961, which were total failures. As there was no more time to be lost the DR decided to turn to the "REKO" option.

The "REKO-IVK" was designed and built by RAW Görlitz ("RAW" means "Reichsbahn-Ausbesserungs-Werk" = DR repair works) and adhered closely to the original Hartmann design but incorporated modern construction technologies. In particular, welding instead of rivetting was applied wherever possible. Thus, both the main and bogie frames, the boiler, the cab, water tanks, and coal bunker were of welded construction. The boiler, built by RAW Halberstadt and designed to produce saturated steam of 14.7 bar pressure, was of similar size to the original boiler but made of one single shell ring (instead of two), of 12 mm sheet thickness. The steam dome had a flat (instead of a round-top) roof and was equipped with two "Ackermann" safety valves. The small steam distribution dome on the boiler front

section was replaced by two feed valves, and the sand dome on the rear boiler section by sand boxes inside the cab. Feedwater was supplied by two steam jets of 60 litres/min capacity.

The first of these engines, No. 99 555, was outshopped in November 1962 and the last, No. 99 590, in November 1967. This latter engine is very probably the "last ever" built compound locomotive in the World. A summary of all the engines is given in Table 2 below while Table 1 presents essential dimensions.

In addition to the 22 new locomotives another eight of the original IVK were reboilered with the new boiler, and were also designated "REKO" by the DR, however, as these have otherwise retained their original Hartmann identity they are not included in table 2.

Similar to their Hartmann predecessors, the REKO-IVK proved to be good engines and have given valuable service for many years. All were renumbered into the DR computer scheme of 1970, and the majority again into the "All-German" DB scheme of 1992, see table 2 for details. The last engines in regular service worked on the Oschatz - Mügeln - Kemlitz branch until December 1993 when this line was sold to a private company, and subsequently dieselised.

No less than eighteen of the REKO-IVK survive today, both in DB AG ownership and at private owners, with eight of them in working order (Table 2). The working engines see occasional use on DB AG "tradition" trains on the Radebeul-Radeburg line, on the private Döllnitz Railway (Mügeln), and on two museum lines at Jöhstadt and Schönheide, (for details consult the DB "Kursbuch"). These locomotives do not usually display the 1992

A rare sight is a IVK displaying her new "All-German" number but two examples were found at Mügeln shed on 24-09-1992, then still under DR management. To the left stands 099 705-6, then a regular Mügeln loco, while to the right the green "tradition" loco 099 701-5 visiting from Radebeul for a steam festival carries cab plates only. As another regular loco had failed that day, the noble tradition loco had offhand been taken to freight work. Today 099 705-6 ex 99 564 has become the second DB "tradition" IVK and has joined 099 701 at Radebeul. The latter is better known by her "tradition" number, "Royal Saxon State Rwy. 132", although she was built as recently as 1963!
Photo: Dr. G. Koch

"All-German" numbers but instead carry their former DR numbers. DB "tradition" locomotive No. 099 701 is painted green and numbered "Royal Saxon State Rwy 132" although she is not an original Hartmann-built "Royal Saxon" but instead a DR product of 1963.

Literature:

G. Moll, R.Scheffler, Die Sächsische IVK (The Saxon IVK), EK-Verlag, Freiburg 1992.

Table 1. Essential dimensions of the DR class REKO-IVK, 0-4+4-0T, gauge 750 mm, built Görlitz 1962-67.

Coupled wheels diameter	760 mm	Boiler dimensions:	
Bogie wheelbase	1,400 mm	Inside diameter	946 mm
Total wheelbase	6,200 mm	Number of tubes	100
Length over buffers	9,000 mm	Tube length	3,500 mm
Weight in working order	29.0 t	Tube diameter, inside	39.5 mm
Coal capacity	1.0 t	Tube diameter, outside	44.5 mm
Water capacity	2.4 m^3	Heating area, firebox	3.9 m^2
Tractive effort	42.2 kN	Heating area, tubes	43.4 m^2
Max. speed	30 km/h	Heating area, total evaporative	47.3 m^2
High pressure cylinders, bore/stroke	240 x 380 mm	Grate area	1.0 m^2
Low pressure cylinders, bore/stroke	400 x 380 mm	Boiler pressure	14.7 bar

Freight on the Saxon narrow gauge was preferrably handled in standard gauge wagons loaded on narrow gauge "Rollbock" piggyback transporters. Loco No. 99 1582-8 is seen crossing the Zschopau bridge near Wolkenstein on the Jöhstadt branch, just below the confluence of the Zschopau and Pressnitz rivers, 3rd May 1980. Photo: *Dr. G. Koch*

Table 2. REKO-IVK locomotives built new by DR Görlitz Works.

Number	Date	Renumbered DR 1970	Renumbered DB 1992	Present Owner and State
99 516	Nov 1963	99 1516-6	-	Retired 1975, monument Rothenkirchen
99 534	Aug 1967	99 1534-9	-	Retired 1975, monument Geyer
99 539	May 1963	99 1539-8	099 701-5	DB tradition loco, Radebeul, working
99 542	Mar 1963	99 1542-2	099 702-3	Mus. Jöhstadt, working
99 555	Nov 1962	99 1555-4	-	Retired 1977, monument Sölmnitz
99 561	Oct 1967	99 1561-2	099 703-1	Döllnitzbahn, Mügeln, working
99 562	Feb 1964	99 1562-0	099 704-9	Stored Saxon Rwy. Mus. Hilbersdorf
99 563	Jan 1964	99 1563-8	-	Retired 1978, scrapped
99 564	Dec 1962	99 1564-6	099 705-6	DB tradition loco, Radebeul, working
99 566	May 1964	99 1566-1	-	Stored Saxon Rwy. Mus. Hilbersdorf
99 574	Jul 1964	99 1574-5	099 707-2	Döllnitzbahn, Mügeln, working
99 582	Jul 1965	99 1582-8	099 708-0	Mus. Jöhstadt, working
99 583	Sep 1965	99 1583-6	-	Retired 1979, scrapped
99 584	Jan 1964	99 1584-4	099 709-8	Döllnitzbahn, Mügeln, working
99 585	Nov 1964	99 1585-1	099 710-6	Mus. Schönheide, working
99 586	Dec 1964	99 1586-9	099 711-4	Retired 1993, monument Radebeul
99 587	Nov 1964	99 1587-7	-	Retired 1974, scrapped
99 590	Nov 1967	99 1590-1	-	Mus. Jöhstadt, working
99 594	May 1963	99 1594-3	-	Sold 1976, stored Ochsenhausen Mus. Rwy.
99 601	Sep 1967	99 1601-6		Retired 1974, scrapped
99 606	Sep 1964	99 1606-5	099 712-2	Ret. 1993, preserved DB Traffic Mus. Nürnberg
99 608	May 1964	99 1608-1	099 713-0	DB Freital-Hainsberg shed, working

Remark: The "missing" locomotive in the All-German 1992 number scheme, No. 099 706-4, is Hartmann-built IVK ex-DR No. 99 568 / 99 1568-7, works No. Hartmann 3450/1910, reboilered at RAW Görlitz June 1964, now on the Jöhstadt Museum line, the only original Hartmann IVK surviving in working order.

Oschatz - Mügeln was the last of the Saxon narrow gauge branches where the "Heberlein" rope brake was used - indeed this device called the "clothes line" persisted locally until 1987, before being displaced by the vacuum brake. On 12th May 1983 REKO-IVK 99 1562-0 approaches Mügeln with a formidable train of standard gauge wagons on "Rollbock" transporters. Photo: Michael Koch.

D.R.N.G. An East German Narrow Gauge Selection

Photographs as credited

Spreewaldbahn 2-6-0T 99.5633 shunting at Straupitz, north of Cottbus in June 1966. The loco, Jung 2519 of 1917, was preserved four years later on the Museumbahn Bruchhausen-Vilsen. Photo: Dipl.-Ing. Klaus Kieper.

99.5633 had until 1954 carried DR number 99.5631, and prior to DR ownership had worked on the Pillkaller Kleinbahn as No. 23. In a typical DR narrow gauge scene a standard gauge wagon is riding on 'rollbocken'. Photo: Dipl.-Ing. Klaus Kieper.

2-10-2T 99.7246-4 arrives at Kirchstrasse station on the metre gauge Wernigerode line in the Harz mountains, on 26th August 1995.

Photo: D. Trevor Rowe.

A metre gauge Mallet 0-4-4-0T, 99.5622 at the head of a mixed train at Altenplein on 23rd May 1966. The loco is one of a pair built by Vulcan of Stettin in 1902 and 1910, originally supplied to the Franzburger Kreisbahnen. Photo: D. Trevor Rowe.

Standard Saxon Railways 750 mm gauge 0-10-0T 99.713 near "Weißes Roß" on the Radebeul - Radeburg line with a regular passenger train, 2nd February 1996. Photo: Joachim Stübben.

On a wintry 1st February 1996, 2-10-2T 099 727-0 hurries along the Freital - Kipsdorf line near Rabenau. Photo: Joachim Stübben.

The 1997 'Bundesgardenshau'

By Joachim Stübben

All photographs by the author

The 'Bundesgartenshau', which could be translated in to English as 'Federal Gardening Exposition', takes place every two years in a different town, and is more than just a flower show. It includes waterworks, sound and light installations, playgrounds and so on, and involves cultural events. For the railfan the 1997 exposition included two interesting features: a monorail and special trains on a conventional line.

The Bundesgartenshau took place at Gelsenkirchen, a city in the Ruhrgebiet, an area between Duisburg and Dortmund traditionally marked by coal mining and heavy industry. The place chosen for the exposition was the grounds of a coal mine named 'Nordstern' (Northern Star), which had been closed down, and so allowed advantage to be taken of a vast area of land, incorporating the mine buildings and waste stone dump as features. As the economic value of coal mining has drastically sunk in the last thirty years, interest in the preservation of the industrial heritage has increased, and several former mines and steel works are now used as art galleries, restaurants, theatres and concert halls, as well as technical museums.

The show's monorail was a circular line with two stations. Eight electric trains were constantly humming along their track at a height of up to 12 metres above the ground, and passengers did not have to wait more than two minutes for a train. On their journey the trains crossed the Emscher river twice and ran through two halls within the colliery complex.

0-6-0T 'Theo 4' passes the abandoned buildings of the Zollverein coal mine with a special train on 23rd August 1997.

The conventional line ran between Nordstern and Zollverein, another closed down mine, about 7 km away at Essen. Trains were operated by diesel hydraulic V200.135 and three different steam locomotives: ELNA type 2-6-0 BLE 146, preserved 2-6-0 no. 24 009, and 0-6-0T 'Theo 4' built in 1949 by the nearby Krupp works, Essen. Among these, 'Theo 4' fitted the industrial envicoment the bast, as it represented a kind of locomotive which used to do much of the shunting work at coal mines and iron & steel works.

For the railway photographer the mining facilities provided interesting backgrounds: pithead gears, bunkers and a loading point (still in use) to which waste stone from the pits is hauled by rail. Perhaps such a mining railway at a garden show might be an inspiration to garden rail enthusiasts.....

D.R.G. Experimental Locomotives
by Keith Chester

TURBINE LOCOMOTIVES

The introduction of the Schmidt superheater was the last significant improvement of the classic Stephenson piston-driven locomotive. A possibility for further partial improvement of the degree of effectiveness was seen in the better exploitation of the temperature gradient during the expansion of steam. The complete expansion of steam to atmospheric pressure was only possible in a steam turbine: the use of turbines, it was hoped, would offer further improvements vis à vis piston locos. The uniform torque ensured in every position a sure and shock-free setting off from standing still, whilst the absence of reciprocating masses eased the problem of balancing the wheels to avoid additional wheel pressure (hammer-blow), thus reducing wear and tear on the track.

Because of its precarious economic situation after World War One, the DRG began to experiment with turbine locomotives relatively late, but could draw on experiments made elsewhere before the First World War, such as in Italy, Sweden and Switzerland.

T18.1001 (Krupp-Zoelly)

Krupp proposed to the D.R.G. a design for a locomotive based on the Swiss turbine loco SBB 1801. The outcome was a Zoelly design with a 4-6-2 wheel arrangement designated as an express loco, delivered by Escher-Wyss Co. (Zürich). The leading bogie had 1,000 mm diameter wheels and the trailing wheels were of 1,250 mm diameter. Because of anticipated higher revolutions the driving and coupled wheels were limited to 1,650 mm.

The turbine and layshaft unit was located under the smokebox, above the front bogie, and consisted of separate forward and reverse turbines as a turbine can only operate in one direction. The six-stage forward turbine developed 2,000 hp at 6,800 r.p.m. (at a speed of approximately 85 kph), and with additional jets, 2,800 hp. The reverse turbine had only a 3-stage crab/sliding

weight. The two turbines were in separate housings mounted either side of gears, the forward turbine on the right (as viewed in the direction of travel), and the reverse on the left. A normal riveted boiler was fitted, and a smokebox in original form divided into double-winged intermediate doors.

The tender, type 2'2'T19.5, fitted with condensing equipment, was mounted on two 4-wheel bogies. The forward part was for up to 6.5 tonnes of coal, with water carried underneath, and the larger rear part contained the condensers.

On completion the loco was extensively tested at the Krupp testing plant, first checking the functioning of the auxiliary machine and then the performance of the main turbines. As steam production and fuel consumption values were not below those of a good piston loco, it was evident that a part of the power was being lost. It was determined that 75.5 hp of the reverse turbine, running in a vacuum, was being consumed in the compression of air. Modifications reduced this loss to 44.5 hp.

The L.V.A. (Locomotive Testing Plant/Institute) at Grunewald received the locomotive in 1928 and began testing on the Burg - Potsdam line with a braking loco, at speeds of 60, 80, and 100 kph. At 1,200 to 1,300 hp and with a coal usage of 0.75 kg per hp per hour, fuel savings of 40% compared to a class 39 (Prussian P.10) and 25% against a class 01 were recorded. According to the terms of the contract, fuel consumption of the turbine loco had to be below that of the most modern piston locomotive at the time of construction, meaning effectively the class 39, as the 01s came a bit later.

In December 1928 and January 1929, T18.1001 ran on trial in the long-distance express diagram between Berlin and Bremen, a distance of 400 km, with stops at Stendal and Hannover. Even with loadings of 580 tonnes, the schedule was easily kept, sometimes even cut, because of the good setting off and acceleration characteristics of the locomotive.

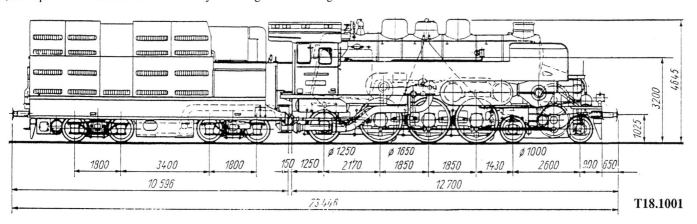

T18.1001

After the trial, the reverse turbine was replaced by a starting up and shunting turbine. The starting up turbine, which automatically switched out at 30 kph, worked on a reversing gear, which by switching enabled the loco to operate in a reverse direction.

T18.1001 was allocated to Hamm M.P.D. and ran with classes 01 and 39 on heavy express diagrams between Aachen - Köln - Hannover, fulfilling her duties without any complaint, but in 1940 she was hit by a bomb in Hamm station. The planned repair at Krupp's factory didn't, however, take place as the loco was unfortunately destroyed in a further bombing raid.

T18.1002 (Maffei)

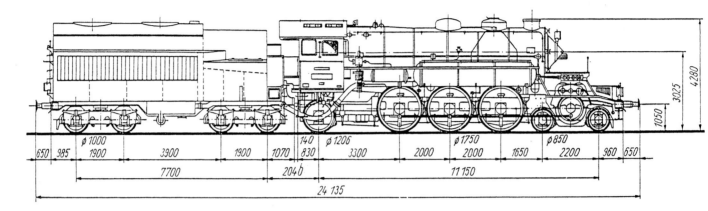

Maffei was given an order to build the second turbine locomotive in September 1924, with a requirement for a maximum speed of 120 kph, and the ability to haul a heavy express at 100 kph on level track.

The first design was for a high pressure piston loco with a low pressure turbine which would switch in later, but the option was then taken for a 100% turbine drive. Originally output was to be that of a class 18³ (Bavarian class S3/6 Pacific), but by increasing axle loading to 20 tonnes the output was increased.

The boiler was of normal riveted construction, with tubes 5,200 mm long and a preheater on each side between the cab and condenser. the last boiler ring was coned. Steam pressure was set at 22 bar (323.4 p.s.i.), and the anticipated savings enabled the boiler to be shortened so that, as on the Krupp loco, there was room for the turbine unit over the front bogie. Externally the Maffei machine differed from the Krupp by having the primary condensers fitted along the frames, underneath the running board either side, whereas on the Krupp these were located across the frames, under the boiler.

In the original form, the forward and reverse turbines were located in a joint housing and drove a shaft via the double layshaft lying near the frames. The main condensing apparatus

was located in the tender, type 2'2'T24, with up to 7 tonnes of coal.

Trials at LVA Grunewald showed that in spite of a higher boiler pressure, the Maffei loco was less economical to operate than the Krupp, and the reason for this was similar - losses through the reverse turbine and excessive steam consumption by the auxiliary machine. The Maffei loco was rebuilt in a similar way to the Krupp - instead of a separate reverse turbine, an additional shunting turbine with gears for forward and reverse was fitted.

T18.1002 was delivered to the D.R.G. on 18th March 1929, and after further trials at LVA Grunewald, went to München Hbf M.P.D., where it was used on expresses and semi-fasts on the routes Munich - Wurzburg and Munich - Lindau. By 1934 the loco had travelled 60,000 km. With the high pressure boiler per se, there were no problems, but owing to the need for frequent repairs and rebuilding of the other units, it was necessary to reduce the high steam consumption of the auxiliary machine.

Damaged by bombing in 1943, T18.002 was withdrawn on 6th October 1943. The boiler was put on the frames of a class 52 and served in Munich Freimann and Ingolstadt loco works as a testbed for boiler safety valves until scrapped in 1961.

T38.3255: P8 WITH EXHAUST STEAM BOOSTER TENDER

One way of improving the thermal efficiency of the steam locomotive is to use the steam expanded to atmospheric pressure. A difficulty here is that it is physically impossible to find room on a locomotive for a cylinder of the required size within the confines of the normal loading gauge, and it is necessary to install turbines either separately for the low-

pressure expansion, or for the total expansion area. For the complete de-pressurisation of the steam a condenser is switched in later.

Together with Dr. Zoelly of the DRB, Henschel developed a piston-turbine locomotive, i.e. a piston steam locomotive with an

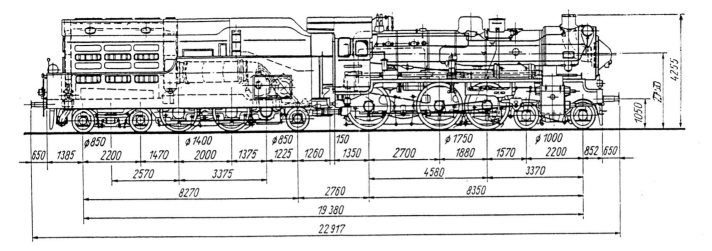

T38.3255

exhaust steam turbine which switched in later. To this end a P8 was rebuilt and a booster tender was constructed. To avoid moving vacuum pipes between locomotive and tender, the turbine condenser and return cooler were all located on the tender.

The booster tender had a 2-4-4 wheel arrangement, with a three-stage forward turbine and a reverse turbine working on the same shaft. As originally in the T18s, this operated in the forward direction in a vacuum and was automatically closed by valves to avoid ventilation losses. The turbines started up when the piston engine exhausted steam.

The tender was completed by Henschel at Kassel in October 1927 and was coupled to an appropriately rebuilt P8 - little actual rebuilding of the locomotive was involved. Suction to draw the hot gases from the firebox through the boiler tubes had to be produced by a fan; the exhaust pipes to the turbine were at the height of the motion.

The first run with a load of 400 tonnes was on 22nd November 1927 between Kassel and Marburg, and a further trial with 480 tonnes took place in December between Kassel and Nordhausen on an express diagram. After some wearisome rebuilding, the locomotive was sent to LVA Grunewald for trials, and finally to Kassel MRD. Both on trial and in service at Kassel the locomotive showed some fundamental deficiencies. As with the Krupp & Maffei turbine locomotives, power losses through the

HIGH-PRESSURE LOCOMOTIVES

In 1922 Fuchs had pressed for a thermal improvement of the steam locomotive. This led to building of the turbine Pacifics T18.1001/2 and the Henschel rebuild of P8 38.3255. Further experiments were carried out with the Schmidt-Henschel high pressure loco H17.206 (dual pressure 60 and 14 bar, rebuilt from an S10²), and the Schwartzkopf-Löffler 4-6-2 H02.1001. A condensing turbine 4-8-2T was designed by Henschel in 1924, but not constructed.

air compression works of the free running reverse turbine were too great. The reverse turbine was therefore switched off from the shaft, as the piston locomotive alone sufficed for reverse. The auxiliary machine was altered from saturated to superheated steam, and this was later further modified to exhaust steam, as the performance characteristic was too unfavourable due to the high consumption of superheated steam by the auxiliary machine.

Further tests at LVA Grunewald showed a 10 per cent rise in performance over the first trial. AT the top of its performance range, the locomotive used 30 per cent less coal than a normal P8; in the middle there was no noticeable difference, and at low level performance fuel consumption was higher than a normal P8. The T38 achieved its best performance at the beginning of the 1930s, when it ran in a diagram with three P10s (DB class 39, 2-8-2), achieving equal output for equal power consumption.

But in the long term there were more and more failures, so that the locomotive had no advantage over a normal piston locomotive. In 1937 the loco was rebuilt to its original condition and coupled to a normal tender. The exhaust steam turbine tender was scrapped. As a normal P8, 38.3255 was in service at Minden MPD until sold for scrap on 20th March 1961. Because of the high costs of (1) building the booster tender, (2) rebuilding a piston locomotive, and (3) general maintenance, this remained the only experiment with a combined piston locomotive and an exhaust steam turbine.

H02.1001

H02.1001 was conceived of as part of the class 01/02 Pacifics programme, to enable a ready comparison to be made with a standard Pacific. The 'H' stands for Hochdruck - high pressure. The multi-pressure boiler supplied steam at an amazing 120 bar, 1,750 psi, to two outside cylinders of very small diameter, and these exhausted into a single low-pressure compound cylinder between the frames.

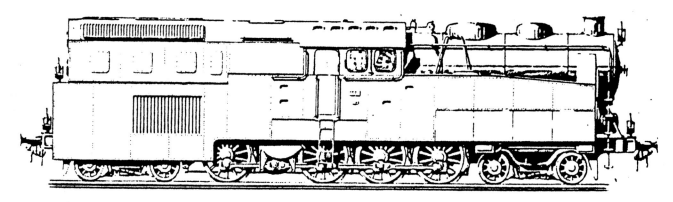

The Proposed 4-8-4T Condensing Turbine Locomotive (1924)

Schwartzkopf guaranteed in the contract a coal saving of 42% with H02.1001 over a standard 01. The contract also included a clause whereby Schwartzkopf was to supply a standard 01 if H02.1001 proved inadequate after sufficient trials. The number 01.011 was long held free for the high-pressure locomotive, but the slot was later filled by a rebuilt class 02. In the event Schwartzkopf provided the D.R.G. with an 03 Pacific.

Trials of H02.1001 followed with great interest and hope, however, the loco never fulfilled its promise, proving even less successful on trial than H17.206, which itself was less than a 100% success. This was for the same reasons as experiments in France and in England ('Fury') - there was little advance over a conventional, low pressure locomotive, but a great increase in costs.

On trial it proved useful to couple the braking loco immediately behind the dynamometer car and H02.1001, so that in the case of (the expected) failure it was possible to tow both away quickly and thus keep the main line clear for normal traffic. H02.1001 was never actually owned by the D.R.G.

H02.1001

19.1001. Photo: Dr. Günther Scheingraber.

The class 05 4-6-4 of 1935 represented the physical limits of conventional locomotive design in Germany: it was not possible to produce an engine capable of running faster. The wheel diameter was at its maximum within the loading gauge and the axle rpm. was limited by piston speed.

19.1001 was a break from the conventional locomotive. It was an attempt initiated in 1934 to exploit individually driven axles, already proven a success by a whole series of electric locos (E04, E16, E17, E18, E19). Steam motors drove four independently powered axles, plus there were two unpowered pony and trailing axles. This arrangement might best be described in the same terms as an electric locomotive, as a 1Do1.

19.1001 had a riveted boiler, (based on the Einheitslok (standard) boiler of the class 44 2-10-0), with an all-welded firebox mounted on frames 70 mm thick. The pony truck and leading powered axle were joined in a Krauss-Helmholtz bogie, whilst the unpowered trailing axle was in a Bissel truck. Knorr brakes were fitted. The external appearance was dictated by streamlining similar to the classes 01^{10} and 03^{10}, and a standard tender of type 2'3T38 was attached, also streamlined.

Each powered axle was driven by its own individual steam motor, a 2-cylinder reciprocating steam machine with the simple-expansion cylinders set in V-formation at 90°. For axles 1 and 3 this was situated on the left hand side, for 2 and 4 on the right hand side. The motors had a 300 mm stroke and the same, 300 mm, diameter, and were sprung. The relative movement between the crankshaft of the motor and the axle was balanced by joints known as Gelenk-Kupplingen.

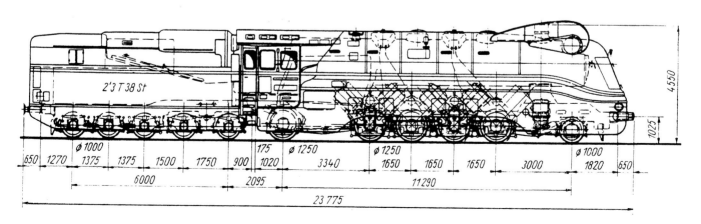

As with electric locomotives with individually driven axles, speed was dependent upon the diameter of the powered wheels, which at 1,250 mm was somewhat under the normal size for a freight loco. The number of revolutions per minute for the motor was identical to that of the axles, meaning 800 rpm at 175 kph.

Boiler pressure was 20 bar (285 psi), and axle loading 18 tonnes, thus enabling 19.1001 to be used on all main lines. On trial the loco used an excessive amount of steam and had difficulty in starting to move. The cause of this was the piston rings sitting too tightly in the grooves, which meant they were not steam tight. Modifications to the piston rings reduced steam

use by 12% and the loco was able to start normally. 19.1001 ran very smoothly, even at high speeds - up to 180 kph on test.

Because of World War 2 it was not possible to make many high speed runs. On 30th April 1943 19.1001 was placed on a normal express diagram, running from Berlin to Hamburg and return. Until 1944 she hauled many heavy expresses Berlin - Hamburg - Osnabrücke, but in August 1944 19.1001 was damaged in a bombing raid and set aside. Later she was captured at Göttingen by advancing U.S. troops, who ordered Henschel to repair her. In 1945, 19.1001 was shipped to the USA as war booty and exhibited at Monroe (Virginia) before being cut up in 1950.

.Coming shortly from LOCOMOTIVES INTERNATIONAL:

BROADER THAN BROAD

Hitler's Great Dream; Three Metre Gauge Rails Across Europe

by Robin Barnes

This is a short account of perhaps the most extraordinary railway project ever conceived. The reader interested primarily in locomotives may consider much of the material extraneous; if so, the writer is sorry, but makes no apologies. After all, railway locomotives never are designed in a vacuum, external influences constantly being at play, and to appreciate properly why such locomotives as are described here were proposed, it is necessary to understand at least something of the surrounding circumstances. He feels also that a reasonably comprehensive outline is of value, as the subject, which surely must be of interest to most railway enthusiasts however they view it, has received little attention in the English language.

The reader is left to form his or her own opinion; the writer asks only that he or she does not confuse fascination with admiration.

Contents:

The story of the Breitspur-Fernbahn, illustrated with the technical drawings, sketches and paintings of Robin Barnes, was originally published as a series of articles, but is now to be released as a Locomotives International special edition.

A Last Glance West and East

Photographs as credited

Preserved 4-6-4T 62.015

62.015 was the last of a series of fifteen 4-6-4Ts built by Henschel in 1928, incorporating standard design features and components, following closely the contemporary Pacifics. No side tanks were fitted, as good stability was required for working passenger trains at speed, so the water was carried under the bunker at the rear.

Right: On the rainy morning of 20th October 1996, 62.015 leaves Bonn at the head of a special from Köln to Kreuzberg and Ahr. Photo: Joachim Stübben.

Below: 62.015 moves its train out of Radebeul Ost, bound for Meissen on 23rd August 1995. The baggage van behind the loco in both photos appears to be the same one, perhaps the support coach.
Photo: D. Trevor Rowe.

DR 2-10-0 50.3616 crosses Markersbach viaduct on a farewell trip on 20th September 1997, prior to closure of the bridge. No doubt the axle weight restriction determined the choice of loco on this structure. Photo: Dr. Günter Koch.

On the Eisenbahnfreunde Zollernbahn preservation line D.E.V.-owned G12 2-10-0 58.311 storms the bank from Epfenhofen with four-wheel coaching stock on 19th April 1987. Photo: D. Trevor Rowe.

Saxon class XII H2

The Saxon State Railways had 159 of these 4-6-0s, often referred to as the 'Saxon P8s', really a misnomer as they were a totally different design. The Belpaire boiler was at a slightly higher pressure, and supplied smaller cylinders. The driving wheels were also smaller, thus giving a higher tractive effort - more suited to service in the hills of Saxony.

Preserved Saxon 4-6-0 no. 38.205 steams past DR diesel 228 805-8 at Brandenburg with a special train from Berlin to Rathenow on 16th April 1885.
Photo: Joachim Stübben.

38.246, one of the later engines with a higher running plate, represents the class in everyday use. The loco is seen in 1983 running tender-first near Wolkenstein on what would today be regarded as priceless vintage rolling stock!
Photo: D. Trevor Rowe.

52.8157, Oberoderwitz 1983.
(D. Trevor Rowe)

The Authors:

A number of authors have shared their expertise or provided photographs for this edition, many of whom are already well known through other work published in 'Locomotives International' magazine and elsewhere.

Paul Catchpole

Having been raised next to the Great Western main line from Birmingham to Paddington during the last decade of steam, the first venture to see railways not only beyond Britain, but even beyond G.W.R. territory was a trip to Germany. Travels to other parts of Europe followed in the final years of working steam. A visit to Czechoslovakia in June 1989 triggered several years of research culminating in 'The Steam Locomotives of Czechoslovakia', published independently by the author in 1995. Paul Catchpole now edits and publishes 'Locomotives International' magazine.

Keith R. Chester

A frequent contributor to 'Locomotives International', and editor/author of the book 'East European Narrow Gauge', Keith Chester is based in Vienna as a university lecturer. He is best known for his research and photography in central Europe, and travels frequently in that area in pursuit of such work, but has also covered steam traction in southern Africa, India, South America, China and Indonesia, and can truly be considered a World authority on the subject.

Paul Cotterell

Paul Cotterell lives and works in Israel, writing during his spare time for 'Harakevet', the journal of railways in the Middle East. He also travelled extensively in Europe and North America during the 1960s and 1970s, and has contributed substantially to the archives of 'Locomotives International', leaving a legacy of this era for the future.

Ian G.T. Duncan

Ian Duncan has been writing about and taking photographs of steam in Britain, Europe and beyond since the 1940s, and has generated much interest with a first-hand illustrated account of the only Brotan-boilered locomotive ever to work in Britain and a series of feature articles on steam at work in the various countries of Scandinavia, through which he travelled in the late 1940s.

Wolfgang Ewers

Living in Germany and having made several visits to Wangerooge for pleasure and for study, author Wolfgang Ewers has written substantially on the history of the island's railways for this book, and this is believed to be the first time a full description has appeared in the English language.

Dr. Günter Koch

Between his many and extensive travels in South America Dr. Koch finds time to write articles and provide photographs for several journals, including 'Locomotives International' as well as German magazines. He has a great fondness for Saxony, to which regular visits are made for steam on the narrow-gauge lines, and about which he is a recognised authority.

D. Trevor Rowe

Another well-known personality and a writer/photographer whose experience spans many countries across the World, and who passes on his knowledge as a regular contributor to the magazine. Mr. Rowe's travels in West Germany in the 1950s/60s formed the basis for a series of articles on narrow gauge and private railways, and he has had a number of books published on other railway subjects, with an accent particularly on narrow gauge themes and more recently looking at railways in Spain.

Joachim Stübben

Joachim Stübben grew up in Germany, but now lives and works in Romania. He is one of today's great steam photographers, whose work is recognisable by the combination of balanced composition and full locomotive action. In this book he writes for the first time about his roots in the Ruhr and shares some of his earliest images. As well as photography in Germany and Romania, Joachim Stübben has also captured the essence of Cuba's sugar mill railways, and is a rising star to look out for in the future.

Photo Credits:

The photographers whose work is published in this edition are credited in the captions.

Other publications from *LOCOMOTIVES INTERNATIONAL*

EAST EUROPEAN NARROW GAUGE by Keith Chester   **£14.95**
116 pages 215 x 270mm, laminated card cover, extensively illustrated with black and white photographs and diagrams.

None of the material in this book has been published previously, and this work from a known authority on the subject significantly expands the information available on narrow gauge steam. Detailed profiles include the Hungarian MÁV class 490 0-8-0T, Kolomna 0-8-0s in Estonia, the Polish class Px48 0-8-0, and the Russian and Chinese Pt-4 0-8-0s. Other chapters cover Die Kleinbahn Des Kreises Jerichow 1, the Upper Silesian Narrow Gauge Railway, forestry railways in the former Jugoslavia, the Slovakian Hronec forestry line, and Romanian State Railways (CFR) narrow gauge lines and locomotives.   ISBN 1-873150-04-0

THE STEAM LOCOMOTIVES OF CZECHOSLOVAKIA by Paul Catchpole   **£16.95**
196 pages 210 x 290mm, hardback colour cover, 92 b&w photos, over 100 technical drawings, most reproduced to modelling scales.

Researched over five years, including translating Jindřich Bek's 'Atlas Lokomotiv', we are given a review of each steam type that ran on the ČSD. The first chapter provides a general history of the railways, and each subsequent chapter starts with an overview of the railway or period concerned. The first three sections detail locomotives absorbed from constituent state railways, followed by sections covering major private railways. Separate chapters describe the period 1918-38 with its classic designs, the legacies of the wartime years 1938-45, and the ultimate development of main-line steam. Narrow gauge locos and steam railcars are included, and an easy reference by class number forms the index.   ISBN 1-873150-14-8

RED NORTE: The Story of State-Owned Railways In The North of Chile by Ian Thomson   **£14.95**
130 pages 215 x 275mm, hardback, colour cover, 72 b/w photographs, 4 maps.

'Red Norte' means 'Northern Network', a term applied to a metre gauge line which commences at La Calera, some 100 kms north west of Santiago and terminates 2000 kms further north at the port of Iquique. Parts of the Red Norte were at one time owned and operated by British companies, but this book could not have been written solely by research in British, or even Chilean archives. Ian Thomson's work as a transport economist takes him around South America and allows opportunities to study source documents not normally available for public viewing.

The history of 'Red Norte' is recounted right from the beginning up to the present day, with extensive details of motive power and traffic, as well as how it developed in the prevailing economic and geographical environment. Living in Chile has enabled the author to gather information first-hand from employees of the former companies, some of whom have provided priceless old photographs from their personal collections, as this book is their story too.   ISBN 1-900340-05-4

THE "LITTLE" NORTH WESTERN RAILWAY by Donald Binns   **£10.95**
Skipton North Jnc - Lancaster, & The Ingleton - Low Gill Branch
90 pages 215 x 270mm, laminated card cover, 140 black & white photos, maps, and diagrams.

A detailed history is provided in eleven chapters extensively illustrated with archive photographs. The text includes a working timetable from the 1880s, details of excursion traffic, train services in the 1930s and locomotive information. Each station is illustrated with track diagrams and photographs at various times in its history, as are goods sheds and crossing keepers cottages. The industrial spur and approaches to Lancaster are also covered.   ISBN 0-873150-01-6

'LOCOMOTIVES INTERNATIONAL' is a high quality bi-monthly publication covering British-built steam overseas, and overseas railways in general. It is not a news magazine, but is made up of well researched articles and classic monochrome photo-features, giving a view of railways both broad and narrow throughout the world. Regular contributors include well-known authors such as Keith Chester, A.E. 'Dusty' Durrant, Ian Duncan, D. Trevor Rowe and Ian Thomson, plus others whose specialist or local knowledge provides in-depth reading.

£3.75 per issue, 1-year subscription (6 issues) £21.00

All prices include postage for UK, Europe, & worldwide surface mail (For air mail add 20%)
Payment may be made by cheque/P.O. or by credit card, quoting the card number & expiry date, and with a signature provided.
Order from: Paul Catchpole Ltd., 47 Glenwood Road, Kings Norton, Birmingham, B38 8HE

German interest articles in *Locomotives International* back issues:

Single back issues are available at £3.75 each - £3.30 if ordering three or more.

All prices include postage for UK, Europe, & worldwide surface mail (For air mail add 20%)

Payment may be made by cheque/P.O. or by credit card, quoting the card number & expiry date, and with a signature provided.

Order from: Paul Catchpole Ltd., 47 Glenwood Road, Kings Norton, Birmingham, B38 8HE